Pebble®

Scottish Fold Cats

by Connie Colwell Miller

Consulting Editor: Gail Saunders-Smith, PhD

Consultant: Jennifer Zablotny, DVM
Member, American Veterinary Medical Association

Capstone
press®
Mankato, Minnesota

Pebble Books are published by Capstone Press,
151 Good Counsel Drive, P.O. Box 669, Mankato, Minnesota 56002.
www.capstonepress.com

1 2 3 4 5 6 13 12 11 10 09 08

Library of Congress Cataloging-in-Publication Data
Miller, Connie Colwell, 1976–
    Scottish fold cats / by Connie Colwell Miller.
    p. cm. — (Pebble Books. Cats)
    Includes bibliographical references and index.
    Summary: "Simple text and photographs present an introduction to the Scottish
Fold breed, its growth from kitten to adult, and pet care information" — Provided
by publisher.
    ISBN-13: 978-1-4296-1932-5 (hardcover)
    ISBN-10: 1-4296-1932-5 (hardcover)
    1. Scottish fold cat — Juvenile literature. I. Title.
SF449.S35M55 2009
636.8'22 — dc22   2007051275

Note to Parents and Teachers

The Cats set supports national science standards related to life
science. This book describes and illustrates Scottish Fold cats.
The images support early readers in understanding the text. The
repetition of words and phrases helps early readers learn new
words. This book also introduces early readers to subject-specific
vocabulary words, which are defined in the Glossary section. Early
readers may need assistance to read some words and to use the
Table of Contents, Glossary, Read More, Internet Sites, and Index
sections of the book.

Table of Contents

4

Teddy Bear Cats

Scottish Fold cats have ears that fold down. People say they look like teddy bears.

Scottish Folds have
large round eyes
and short noses.

Scottish Folds can be many colors.
Tabby Scottish Folds are striped.

From Kitten to Adult

Scottish Fold kittens are born with straight ears. Their ears fold down after three or four weeks.

12

Some Scottish Folds' ears
never fold down.
They still make
great pets.

Scottish Folds grow
into medium-sized cats.
Their round bodies
are thick and strong.

Caring for Scottish Folds

Scottish Folds' coats
are short and thick.
They need to be brushed
two or three times
each week.

Scottish Folds' ears
must be cleaned carefully.
A wet cloth works well
to clean them.

Scottish Folds are calm cats. They make wonderful pets.

Glossary

calm — quiet and peaceful

coat — an animal's hair or fur

tabby — a cat with a striped coat

Read More

Barnes, Julia. *Pet Cats.* Pet Pals. Milwaukee: Gareth Stevens, 2007.

Shores, Erika L. *Caring for Your Cat.* Positively Pets. Mankato, Minn.: Capstone Press, 2007.

Internet Sites

FactHound offers a safe, fun way to find Internet sites related to this book. All of the sites on FactHound have been researched by our staff.

Here's how:

1. Visit *www.facthound.com*

2. Choose your grade level.

3. Type in this book ID **1429619325** for age-appropriate sites. You may also browse subjects by clicking on letters, or by clicking on pictures and words.

4. Click on the **Fetch It** button.

FactHound will fetch the best sites for you!

Index

Word Count: 119
Grade: 1
Early-Intervention Level: 12

Editorial Credits
Lori Shores, editor; Renée T. Doyle, set designer; Danielle Ceminsky, book designer;
    Wanda Winch, photo researcher

Photo Credits
Alamy/Interfoto Pressebildagentur, 8
Fox Hill Farms, Norvia Behling/Daniel Johnson, 12
Kimball Stock/Ron Kimball, cover, 6
Peter Arnold/W. Layer, 14
Shutterstock/Ekaterina Cherkashina, 1, 10, 22; s-dmit, 4
Ulrike Schanz Photodesign & Animal Stock, 16, 18, 20